Twenty to

Washi Tape
Cards

Sara Naumann

Search Press

First published in Great Britain 2015

Search Press Limited
Wellwood, North Farm Road,
Tunbridge Wells, Kent TN2 3DR

Text copyright © Sara Naumann 2015

Photographs by Fiona Murray

Photographs and design copyright
© Search Press Ltd 2015

Print ISBN: 978-1-78221-203-4
EPUB ISBN: 978-1-78126-264-1
Mobi ISBN: 978-1-78126-265-8

Suppliers
If you have difficulty in obtaining any of the
materials and equipment mentioned in this
book, then please visit the Search Press website
for details of suppliers: www.searchpress.com

Printed in China

Dedication
*This book is for my mom, Belinda
and Anna – my three favourite
crafting companions!*

Contents

Introduction

Sometimes the most inspiring craft materials are the simplest! Washi tape is one of those – and has fast become one of my go-to supplies for card-making. Available in a fabulous array of colours and patterns, washi tape offers so many possibilities for card designs.

Washi tape is a high-quality decorative tape originally from Japan. You can cut it, tear it, stick it, layer it, fold it, stamp on it, or even add paint, embossing powder or dry embossed texture. Use it as an accent on a card, or the background. You can peel and stick for a quick dash of colour and style – or incorporate stamping and mixed-media techniques for extra fun.

The hardest part about working with washi tape is choosing just one or two rolls. It's easy to get dazzled by all the different patterns available – and it can be downright impossible to pick just a few designs.

My tip is to start with colours you are drawn to, or those you use often in your card-making. Pick a couple of patterns you can use together. It is often helpful to buy a coordinating set of tapes, but do not feel limited to tone-on-tone designs – contrasting colours and patterns can coordinate well, too.

I also suggest at least one solid-colour tape to start. Solids are great between patterns to create visual 'space' and help each pattern stand out. They are also ideal for stamping and heat-embossing techniques.

You can create any of these cards with whichever washi tapes you have to hand. You can always swap my colour combinations and pattern choices for your own favourites. In this book, you will discover dozens of ways to play with a few simple rolls of tape!

Tools and materials

A **paper trimmer** makes it easy to get perfectly straight lines and evenly cut pieces. **Detail scissors** are ideal for cutting around small embellishments.

A **bone folder and ruler** or **scoring blade** for a paper trimmer give crisply scored lines so you can easily fold your paper.

Stamps work beautifully with washi tape and allow you to customise your cards. I use clear acrylic stamps and an acrylic block.

Stencils and **templates** are very versatile. Apply paint or embossing paste through a stencil, or use a pencil to trace a shape with a template, then cut it out.

A **die-cutting/embossing machine** like the Artisan X-plorer™ creates die-cut pieces as well as embossed designs. Run paper through in a plastic **embossing folder** to create texture and dimension. Use **metal dies** to cut paper and cardstock into detailed shapes.

A **heat tool** is used to melt embossing powder, creating a raised stamped image.

Craft punches create circles, scallops and other designs – just slide your paper into the punch, press and remove your cut piece.

I always work on a **craft sheet**. It is non-porous, non-stick and heat-resistant. It protects your work surface while stamping and heat-embossing and cleans up easily.

Washi tape is a decorative sticky tape which comes in many different colours and patterns. It can be semi-translucent and is easy to apply and remove without leaving any adhesive residue. **Coloured and white cardstock** is a must for card-making. White is a basic and makes the pattern on the washi tape stand out. Use lightweight white **paper** (like computer printer paper) when folding or manipulating tape. **Patterned paper** gives instant colour and style to cards. Pages torn from old books can also be fun backgrounds.

You can use **alcohol markers** or **coloured pencils** to fill in **outline stickers**; you can also place the stickers on coloured cardstock, paper or even washi tape and trim around the outside edge with a pair of detail scissors.

I use **double-sided tape** for all paper-to-paper attaching. White **craft glue** is best for gluing and embellishments, and **foam mounting tape** gives layers of dimension.

Use a **permanent inkpad** such as StazOn or Surfacez to stamp on washi tape. Avoid pigment inks, which can smear. Slow-drying **embossing inks**, such as Versamark, are designed for heat-embossing. A **mini brayer** makes it easy to roll ink on to background paper.

Embellishments like **silk flowers**, **brads** (paper fasteners), **buttons** and **ribbons** make easy accents and card focals.

Acrylic paint and **embossing paste** give a mixed-media effect, especially in combination with stencils. Embossing paste is easiest to apply with a **palette knife**. I often use a **cosmetic wedge** to apply paint through stencils.

Basic techniques

Stamping

1 Place the stamp on a clear acrylic block, then apply ink with an inkpad.

2 Stamp the design on to the paper, ensuring that you press firmly and evenly.

3 Clean the stamp with soap and water, then return it to the liner sheet.

Heat embossing

1 Stamp the image with embossing ink and immediately sprinkle with embossing powder. The powder will stick to the wet ink. Tap off excess powder and return to the jar.

2 Use a small dry paintbrush to gently whisk away stray pieces of powder.

3 Set with a heat tool. The powder will melt to create a raised image.

Dry embossing

1 Place the paper in a plastic embossing folder, and sandwich it between the embossing plates.

2 Run it through the embossing machine, following the manufacturer's instructions.

Stencil Flower

Materials:

Washi tape: solid green, yellow floral, green floral

White acrylic paint

Black lacy flower stickers

Black and white cardstock

White and orange ribbon

Blank white card, 12.7 x 16.5cm (5 x 6½in)

Foam mounting tape

Double-sided tape

Masking tape

Lightweight white paper

Tools:

Scallop circle punch 6¼cm (2½in)

Polka dot stencil

Detail cutting scissors

Cosmetic wedge

Instructions:

1 Place seven alternating strips of washi tape vertically on a piece of white card. Trim to 10 x 15¼cm (4 x 6in). Place the circles portion of the stencil on top and hold it in place with masking tape.

2 Use the cosmetic wedge to sponge white paint through the stencil. Lift straight off and clean the stencil immediately. Let the painted paper dry.

3 Use double-sided tape to mount the washi tape paper on black card. Hold white and orange ribbon together, then tie in a knot. Wrap around the washi tape paper, securing the ends to the back. Attach to the left side of the card front.

4 Place two short strips of yellow floral washi tape on the edge of a piece of lightweight white paper. Place the flower sticker on top, positioning just the blossom on the yellow tape. Do not allow the rest of the sticker to adhere to the paper. Use detail scissors to trim away the paper so the blossom is backed with yellow. Repeat with solid green washi tape for the leaves.

5 Punch a scallop circle from white card and attach the flower sticker with foam tape. Punch a scallop circle from black card; foam-tape the white scallop on top, slightly offset. Use foam tape to attach it to the card front.

Paint and Stencil Cupcake

Add emphasis to stencilled circles with black penwork. Simply let the paint dry on the washi tape, then reposition the stencil and trace with a permanent fine-tip pen. This card design also features a cupcake outline sticker coloured with alcohol pens for a bright, festive look.

Rosette Swirl

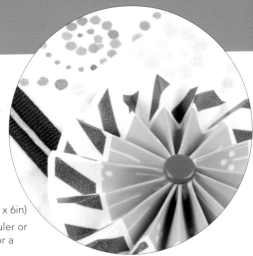

Materials:

Washi tape: green floral and navy stripe

Green ink spray

Navy and white cardstock

White vellum paper

Navy grosgrain ribbon and twine

Navy brads

12.7 x 16.5cm blank white card (5 x 6½in)

Foam mounting tape

Double-sided tape

Craft glue

Masking tape

Lightweight white paper

Cardboard box for spraying into

Kitchen roll

Tools:

Swirly dots stencil 15¼ x 15¼cm (6 x 6in)

Bone folder and ruler or scoring blade for a paper trimmer

Instructions:

1 Place the stencil on top of white cardstock and secure with masking tape. Spray with green ink spray, then blot with kitchen roll. Remove the stencil and clean it. Let the sprayed cardstock dry.

2 Place a strip of green floral and a strip of navy stripe washi tapes on a 3 x 29cm (1¼ x 11⅝in) piece of lightweight white

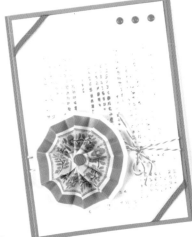

paper. Score every 1cm (³/₈in), then concertina-fold the strip. Glue the ends together and press gently into a rosette. Insert a brad in the centre, with a touch of glue to secure; allow to dry.

3 Cut the sprayed piece to 11.5 x 15cm (4½ x 6in) and mount on navy card with double-sided tape. Position an 8.5cm (3³/₈in)-wide piece of white vellum across horizontally, secure with brads on the right and a light touch of glue on the left where the rosette will go.

4 Hold the navy ribbon and twine together and tie in a knot; wrap around the sprayed piece, securing the ends to the back. Use foam tape to attach the piece to the card front.

5 Use foam tape to attach the rosette to the card front.

Rosette Screen

Use lightweight paper such as printer paper for this technique, in order to get crisp, clean folds. Then experiment with different colours and patterns of washi tape. Here, the floral tape goes in the centre of the rosette, but would look equally pretty on the outer edge.

Dry Embossed Flower

Materials:

Washi tape: solid green, narrow pale green, red with dots, white with striped circles

Black and white cardstock

Black ribbon

Blank white card 12.7 x 16.5cm (5 x 6½in)

White and blue silk flowers

Red brad

Foam mounting tape

Double-sided tape

Tools:

Woven lattice embossing folder

Die-cutting/embossing machine

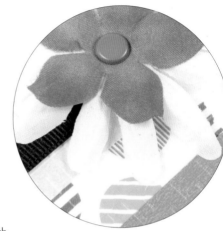

Instructions:

1 Place five alternating strips of washi tape vertically along the right side of a 10 x 14.5cm (4 x 5¾in) piece of white card. Place three alternating strips of washi tape horizontally across the bottom left corner.

2 Place the cardstock into the embossing folder and run through the embossing machine. Remove, then mount on black card with double-sided tape. Wrap black ribbon horizontally across the piece, securing the ends to the back. Glue to the card front.

3 Insert a red brad through blue and white silk flowers. Use foam tape to attach this decoration to the card front.

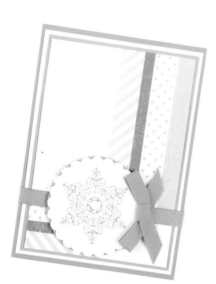

Dry Embossed Snowflakes

This technique gives subtle texture and dimension to your cards. Even better, it makes it easy and inexpensive to mass-produce a batch of cards – perfect if you have a big Christmas card list!

Embossing Paste Hat

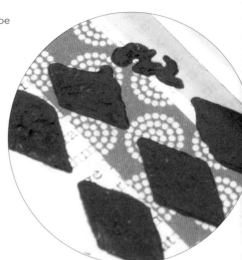

Materials:

Washi tape: red floral circles, solid turquoise, black stripe

Black embossing paste

Book page

White acrylic paint

Bowler hat and moustache stickers

Red and white cardstock

Black inkpad

Black and white gingham ribbon

Blank black card 11.5 x 16cm (4½ x 6¼in)

Foam mounting tape

Double-sided tape

Craft glue

Masking tape

Scrap paper

Tools:

Mini diamond stencil 15¼ x 15¼cm (6 x 6in)

Palette knife

Paintbrush

Instructions:

1 Paint a book page with white acrylic paint. Let it dry, then place five strips of washi tape on top vertically, leaving a small space in between.

2 Place the stencil on top of the book page and secure with masking tape. Use the palette knife to spread a generous amount of embossing paste over the stencil.

3 Lift the stencil straight off the book page and place it on to scrap paper. Use the palette knife to scrape off excess embossing paste from the stencil and return it to the jar. Clean the stencil immediately with soap and water.

4 Let the book page dry, then use double-sided tape to attach it to the card front, leaving a narrow border on each long side.

5 Place the hat and moustache stickers on a piece of white card, 5.5 x 7cm (2¹/₈ x 2¾in) in size. Mount on red card, then use foam tape to mount again on white. Ink the edges using the black inkpad, then use foam tape to adhere to the card front.

6 Tie a knot in a piece of gingham ribbon, then glue as shown.

Camera Embossing Paste

When choosing tape and stencil combinations, remember that circular patterns look great with stripes. Here the chevron washi tape makes a fun striped background for the circle stencil design.

Die-cut Washi Tape

Materials:

Washi tape: semicircles, solid dark purple, solid lavender

White, lavender and yellow cardstock

Turquoise grosgrain ribbon

Purple embossing powder

Embossing inkpad

Blank white card 12.7 x 16.5cm (5 x 6½in)

Blue and yellow silk flowers

Purple brad

Foam mounting tape

Double-sided tape

Craft glue

Tools:

Oblong cutting dies with 'bracket' sides

Die-cutting/embossing machine

Stamp set

Heat tool

Instructions:

1 Place 11 alternating strips of washi tape on white cardstock, then place on the cutting surface with the metal die and run through the die-cutting machine. Die-cut a second piece of plain lavender cardstock and attach the two together with double-sided tape, slightly offset.

2 Die-cut a smaller white cardstock label. Stamp 'Merci' in the centre with embossing ink, then emboss with purple embossing powder. Die-cut the same size label from lavender cardstock and glue the two together, slightly offset. Attach to the larger label with foam tape.

3 Cut 2.5cm (1in) from the front flap of the blank card. Cover the card front with yellow cardstock, leaving a narrow border at the bottom edge. Wrap turquoise ribbon around the card front, securing the ends at the front of the card with double-sided tape. Use foam tape to attach the die-cut piece to the front.

4 Insert a purple brad in yellow and blue flowers, then glue to the card front. Tie a knot in turquoise ribbon and glue it to the right side of the label.

5 Line the inside of the card with lavender cardstock, leaving a narrow border at the bottom edge. Place the semicircles washi tape on white cardstock, trim the edges and glue along the bottom of the card inside, so it will show when the card is closed.

Telephone Die-Cut Washi Tape

Crisp, clean lines and an elegant die-cut shape give this card some retro style – the telephone outline sticker adds a touch of nostalgia. The sticker is backed with white paper before being attached to the card with foam tape.

Stencil and Paint

Materials:

Washi tape: purple/brown patchwork, solid lavender

Green and purple coloured pencils

Blue acrylic paint

Brown and white cardstock

Black inkpad

Blank white card 12.7 x 16.5cm (5 x 6½in)

Double-sided tape

Sheer blue ribbon

Masking tape

Cosmetic wedge

Tools:

Flower stencil 15¼ x 15¼cm (6 x 6in)

Butterfly stamp

Flourish border stamp

Stippling brush

Instructions:

1 Place the stencil on top of white card; secure with masking tape. Use the cosmetic wedge to sponge blue paint through a portion of the stencil. Lift straight off and clean the stencil immediately. Let the painted paper dry.

2 Place varying lengths of torn washi tape strips overlapping a portion of the stencilled area: purple/brown patchwork, lavender and purple/brown stripe.

3 Use black ink to stamp the flourish border design across the paper, on top of the lavender washi tape and the stencilled pattern.

4 Stamp the butterfly with black and colour with pencils.

5 Make a watery mix of blue paint. Use the stipple brush to spatter fine dots of paint over the paper. Allow to dry.

6 Trim the paper to 11 x 15.5cm (4³/₈ x 6in) and mount it on brown card. Tie a knot in a piece of blue ribbon and wrap it around the card, securing the ends to the back of the piece with double-sided tape. Mount it in the centre of the card front.

Bicycle Stencil

Vertical and horizontal strips of washi tape add colour to this minimalist card. The bicycle was heat-embossed with black embossing powder to add extra dimension. The bicycle seat and handlebars are coloured with alcohol pens.

Stamped Feather

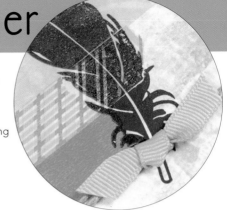

Materials:

Washi tape: solid green, orange/teal patchwork, and solid turquoise

White, green and yellow cardstock

Black inkpad

Alcohol ink refill

Blank white card 12.7 x 16.5cm (5 x 6½in)

Twine

Teal grosgrain ribbon

Foam mounting tape

Double-sided tape

Craft glue

Spray bottle of rubbing alcohol

Tools:

Feathers stamp set

Mini brayer

Craft sheet or palette

Instructions:

1 Squeeze a few drops of alcohol ink refill on to the craft sheet. Spray lightly with rubbing alcohol. Roll the brayer through the mixture, then roll it across a 16 x 10cm (6¼ x 3⁷⁄₈in) piece of white card. Repeat to add as much ink as you like, leaving some areas white. Spray lightly with rubbing alcohol to create a spotty design.

2 Place five torn strips of washi tape horizontally across the cardstock, varying the lengths. Use black ink to stamp the feather on top.

3 Using double-sided tape, mount on a 10.5 x 16.5cm (4 x 6½in) piece of yellow card, then wrap twice with twine. Tie a knot in a piece of teal ribbon, then glue it to the bottom of the feather.

4 Attach a piece of green cardstock, 11.5cm (4½in) wide, across the card front with double-sided tape. Use foam tape to attach the mounted washi tape piece.

Stamped Leaf

This technique works equally well with silhouette and outline stamps. For extra dimension, I filled in the leaf design with clear lacquer, sprinkling with gold highlight embossing glitter while wet. The brayered background uses alcohol ink.

Stencil-cut Flowers

Materials:

Washi tape: neon pink dot and stripe

Teal sheer ribbon

White, pink and cream cardstock

Pink ink spray

Blank white card 12.7 x 16cm (5 x 6¼in)

Foam mounting tape

Double-sided tape

Craft glue

Pencil

Tools:

Blossoms template

Circle punches: 2cm (¾in), 2¼cm (⁷/₈in), 5mm (¼in)

Detail scissors

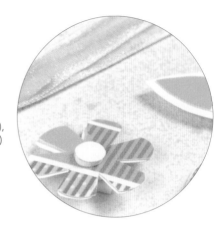

Instructions:

1 Place five strips of washi tape on white cardstock, leaving a 4mm (¹/₈in) space between each one. Turn the paper over and trace a large flower from the template on the back, keeping your pencil on the inner edges of the stencil shape. Cut it out with detail scissors.

2 Trace the same flower on to white cardstock – this time, keep your pencil on the outer edges of the stencil shape to create a slightly larger flower. Cut out and glue the two shapes together.

3 Repeat to create medium and small flower shapes, placing the strips of washi tape slightly closer together.

4 Punch two 2cm (¾in) circles from leftover washi cardstock. Glue each one to a 2¼cm (⁷/₈in) white cardstock circle,

then use foam tape to attach to the centre of the large and medium flowers. Then punch a 5mm (¼in) circle of white cardstock and attach it to the centre of the smallest flower with foam tape.

5 Lightly spray cream cardstock with pink ink spray; when dry, cut to 11 x 16cm (4¼ x 6¼in) and mount the long edges on pink card using double-sided tape. Wrap twice with teal ribbon, securing the ends to the back. Tie another piece of sheer ribbon round the border and tie in a knot. Glue the piece to the card front.

6 Use foam tape to attach the three flowers to the front of the card.

Washi Embossed Flowers

Play with different surface techniques to give your blossoms even more dimension. Here I placed washi tape strips on to book paper, then stamped and heat-embossed an all-over design with gold. The combination lends texture and shine.

Wrapped Chopsticks

Materials:

Washi tape: semicircles, red with dot, green floral

Green baker's twine

Glassine mini envelope 9cm (3½in) square

Chinese book page

White and green cardstock

Blank red card 10 x 21cm (4 x 8¼in)

Wooden chopsticks

Double-sided tape

Craft glue

Instructions:

1 Wrap one chopstick with green floral, semicircles and red with dot washi tapes, placing the tape at an angle, wrapping once or twice around and leaving space between each pattern. Repeat with a second chopstick, wrapping semicircles, red with dot, then semicircles again to cover the entire chopstick.

2 Use craft glue to glue the two chopsticks together, crossed. Wrap with baker's twine and tie in a bow.

3 Cut a piece of green card slightly smaller than the card front. Place a strip of red with dot washi tape on white card and trim, leaving a narrow border on both long edges. Using double-sided tape, attach toward the bottom of the green cardstock piece, then attach to the card front.

4 Cut a piece of Chinese book paper to fit inside the glassine envelope. Place a strip of green floral washi tape on white card and trim, then glue across the envelope. Wrap green baker's twine twice around the envelope, then glue it to the card front.

5 Fold the envelope flap down and secure it with glue. Place a small piece of semicircles washi tape on white card, then trim and glue it to the flap. Tie a bow in the baker's twine and, using craft glue, attach it next to the flap.

6 Use craft glue to secure the chopsticks to the card front.

Washi Tape Toothpicks

Create petite card accents with washi tape flags. Simply place a piece of washi tape around the end of the toothpick and stick the two sides together, then use scissors to cut an inverted 'v'. The gift packages were stamped and embossed, then coloured with alcohol pens.

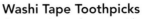

Criss-cross Tape and Flower

Materials:

Washi tape: solid dark purple, plum patterned and narrow plum patterned

Green grosgrain ribbon

Lavender and brown silk flowers

Button

White, lavender and green cardstock

Blank white card 12.5 x 15.5cm (5 x 6in)

Foam mounting tape

Double-sided tape

Craft glue

Instructions:

1 Place five strips of purple washi tape diagonally across a 13.5 x 10cm (5¼in x 4in) piece of white card. Place four strips of patterned plum washi tape diagonally on top, going in the opposite direction.

2 Using double-sided tape, mount the piece on green card and tear the bottom edge, then mount again on lavender. Attach to the card front with the tape.

3 Make a loop from green ribbon and glue it to the card front with craft glue. Glue the lavender flower to the card front, then use foam tape to add the brown flower. Attach the button to the centre with foam tape.

Criss-Cross Washi Tape Floral

Create a bold graphic effect with brightly coloured and patterned washi tapes. Place them at an angle, as with the Flower Card, or set them straight like this one (see left). Add your accents with layers of foam tape to give dimension.

Cross-angle Hearts

Materials:

Washi tape: black houndstooth, black and white dot, narrow pink

Border stickers

Book page

White acrylic paint

Grey grosgrain ribbon

Grey sheer ribbon

White and black cardstock

Embossing inkpad

Glitter embossing powder

Blank black card 11.5 x 16cm (4½ x 6¼in)

Foam mounting tape

Double-sided tape

Craft glue

Tools:

Hearts template

Paintbrush

Pencil

Heat tool

Instructions:

1 Paint a sheet of book paper with two coats of white acrylic paint. Let it dry, then cut slightly smaller than the card front. Wrap with sheer grey ribbon, securing the ends to the back of the paper. Place black border stickers along the top and bottom of the book paper, and just underneath the ribbon. Use double-sided tape to attach to the card front.

2 Use a pencil to trace a large heart shape on to white card. Cut out the shape loosely, then turn it over. Place six strips of washi tape diagonally across the heart shape, beginning at the top right and leaving a small space between each pattern.

3 Cut a straight edge on a piece of washi tape and place it diagonally in the opposite direction, beginning at the bottom right of the heart. Continue to fill the rest of the heart shape with more washi tape, leaving a small space between each one.

4 Turn the heart shape over and then cut carefully along the pattern lines.

5 Trace and cut a medium heart from black card. Ink the edges with embossing ink and sprinkle with glitter embossing powder, then heat set.

6 Trace and cut a small heart from white card. Cut

out the shape loosely, then turn over and place washi tape diagonally across the heart, leaving a small space between each pattern. Turn over and cut along the pattern lines.

7 Stack the three heart shapes with foam tape and attach to the card front with double-sided tape. Tie a bow in grey grosgrain ribbon and use craft glue to secure to the front of the card.

Pincushion Washi Tape

The cross-angle washi tape arrangement can be used to create a card focal, like the heart – or a complete background. The process is the same, but without a template shape. The pincushion stamp was embossed in black, then coloured with alcohol pens.

Square-punched Accents

Materials:

Washi tape: solid green, orange gingham and fruit, green patterned

Orange baker's twine

Buttons

White and green cardstock

Blank white card 12.7 x 16.5cm (5 x 6½in)

Foam mounting tape

Double-sided tape

Craft glue

Tools:

Square punches: 3.75cm (1½in) and 4.75cm (1⅞in)

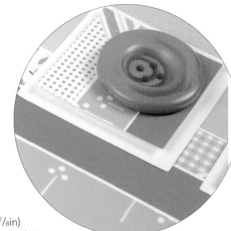

Instructions:

1 Place four strips of washi tape evenly across a piece of white card, leaving a small space between each pattern. Trim, leaving a narrow edge on each long side. Mount on a 10.5 x 17cm (4⅛ x 6¾in) piece of green card and attach to the front of the blank card with double-sided tape.

2 Place three strips of washi tape on white card, leaving a small space between each pattern. Punch three 3.75cm (1½in) squares. Then punch three 4.75cm (1⅞in) squares of white card. Use foam mounting tape to stack the washi tape squares on to the white squares.

3 Wrap baker's twine around the fold of the blank card and tie in a bow at the top. Attach the punched squares evenly along the right side of the card front with double-sided tape. Use craft glue to attach a button in the centre of each square.

Red and Blue Accents

The square trio layout looks just as good as a horizontal card. Change the washi tape colours and patterns, substituting a narrow washi tape between two standard widths for a little variety.

Washi Background

Materials:

Washi tape: red houndstooth, narrow blue

Butterfly stamp

Blue embossing inkpad

Embossing powder

White, navy and red cardstock

Blank white card 12.7 x 16.5cm (5 x 6½in)

Foam mounting tape

Double-sided tape

Tools:

Punches: 6.25cm (2½in) scallop circle, 4.5cm (1¾in) circle

Heat tool

Instructions:

1 Place alternating strips of houndstooth and blue washi tape on white card, leaving a small space between each strip.

2 Cover the card front with navy cardstock. Trim the washi tape piece slightly smaller than the card front and glue in the centre.

3 Place houndstooth washi tape on white card and cut, leaving a slight border. Glue in the centre of a strip of blue card, 4.5cm (1¾in) wide, then mount on white. Glue across the card front, trimming the edges evenly.

4 Stamp and emboss the butterfly on white cardstock, then circle-punch. Punch a red scallop shape and layer with foam tape. Use foam tape to attach it to the front of the card.

Background Leaf

This technique is one of the easiest and most versatile. You can alternate washi strips with different tape patterns – or incorporate patterned paper or paper of your own design. Here I have alternated tape with cardstock that has been coloured with glitter glue. Simply spread the glitter glue on to glossy card, then add tape and metallic border stickers when it is dry.

Woven Washi Strips

Materials:

Washi tape: purple/green patchwork, narrow plum, narrow green

Dragonfly sticker

Gold embossing powder

Embossing inkpad

Patterned paper

Gold metallic ribbon

White cardstock

Purple coloured pencil

Blank white card 12.7 x 16cm (5 x 6¼in)

Foam mounting tape

Double-sided tape

Purple brad

Craft glue

Tools:

Circle punch: 3.5cm (1³/₈in)

Heat tool

Instructions:

1 Place a strip of purple/green patchwork washi tape on white cardstock, then cut to 14.5cm (5¾in) long. Trim one end straight and the other at an angle. Repeat to make two more strips, slightly varying the lengths.

2 Use the same method to make two purple strips and one green strip, cutting them to 13cm (5¼in) long.

3 Cut a piece of green patterned paper slightly smaller than the card front.

4 Arrange the three purple/green patchwork strips as shown, then weave in the purple and green pieces. Adjust so the pieces are spaced as you want, then gently flip them them over and secure on the back with double-sided tape.

5 Use double-sided tape to attach to the green

patterned paper, trimming the green and purple solid washi tape pieces even with the edges. Then attach to the card front.

6 Punch a circle of white cardstock and ink the edges with embossing ink. Sprinkle with gold embossing powder, then heat-set. Add the dragonfly sticker in the centre and colour the wings with purple. Add a brad at the top and a loop of gold ribbon at the back. Use foam tape to attach to the card front.

Woven Washi Heart

Patchwork washi tapes are great for this weaving technique because the patterns change every few centimetres, giving you several patterns on one roll of tape. Feel free to play with the placement of your washi tape strips – you know they will always coordinate. With the plaid patterns, I find it looks best to weave in solid tapes for contrast.

Washi Bunting

Materials:

Washi tape: semicircles, red dot, green dot, narrow blue

Paper flowers

Green brads

Brown, white and green cardstock

Twine

Blank white card 12.7 x 16.5cm (5 x 6½in)

Foam mounting tape

Double-sided tape

Lightweight white paper

Tools:

Toothpick

Instructions:

1 Cut a 14.5 x11.3cm (5¾ x 4³/₈in) piece of brown cardstock and mount on white card, then green, with double-sided tape. Cut a length of twine and secure one end of the twine to the back of the left side.

2 Place a strip of narrow blue and green dot washi tape on a piece of white paper, 10cm (4in) in length. Trim the edges, leaving a narrow border on each long side. Cut one short end even and cut the other end into an inverted 'v' shape. Gently roll the straight-cut edge around the toothpick.

3 Repeat to make a red dot flag, a narrow blue flag, a semicircles flag and another blue/green dot flag, varying the lengths.

4 Place foam tape on the back of each flag, then thread them evenly on the twine and secure to the brown cardstock. Wrap the other end of the twine to the back of the matted cardstock piece and secure.

5 Insert a brad each in three flowers and use foam tape to attach them along the twine. Tie twine between a few of the flags, and at either end.

6 Place red dot washi tape along the top and bottom of the card front. Attach the brown cardstock piece with bunting to the centre of the card front with double-sided tape.

Bunting and Buttons

Create a collage background with patterned papers, then add the bunting flags on top with foam tape. Buttons, silk ribbon and a paper doily border give this piece an eclectic feel.

Ribbon Medallions

Materials:

Washi tape: purple/green patchwork, green floral, narrow green, narrow purple

Patterned papers

Purple baker's twine

Round black stickers

White and brown cardstock

White acrylic paint

Chipboard circle

Green button

Brown solvent inkpad

Blank white card 12.7 x 16.5cm (5 x 6½in)

Foam mounting tape

Double-sided tape

Craft glue

Tools:

Punches: 6.25cm (2½in) scallop circle, 4.5cm (1¾in) circle

Instructions:

1 Cover the card front with brown card. Trim green patterned paper slightly smaller than the card front, ink the edges brown and attach in the centre with double-sided tape. Cut an 11.5 x 15.5cm (4½ x 6in) piece of grey patterned paper and ink the edges. Wrap twice with baker's twine and tie a bow around the two strands. Glue to the card front.

2 Make a ribbon by placing two strips of purple/green patchwork washi tape on white card, leaving a small space between them. Trim, leaving a narrow border on each long edge. Cut one short end to an inverted 'v'.

3 Repeat, placing a narrow strip of green washi tape, a strip of green patterned washi tape and another narrow green strip. Trim as before.

4 Create a third ribbon piece with a strip of narrow green and a strip of narrow purple washi tape.

5 Layer the three washi tape ribbons together with foam tape.

6 To make the ribbon medallion, place green patterned and narrow purple washi tapes on white card, leaving a small space between each strip. Punch into a scallop. Circle punch into a scallop. Circle punch

grey patterned paper, ink the edges brown and glue in the centre. Paint the chipboard circle white and glue on top, then add a button threaded with baker's twine. Use foam tape to glue the medallion to the washi tape ribbons and add to the card front.

7 Place the narrow purple washi tape on white card and trim, creating an inverted 'v' at the end. Add three round black stickers in a line. Gently shape into a wave and glue to the medallion at an angle as shown.

Orange and Green Ribbon Medallion

This ribbon medallion technique looks best when constructed with layers of foam tape – it adds dimension and helps each element stand out. If you are concerned it might get damaged in the mail, simply nest a piece of bubble wrap underneath the edges of the medallion or place the card in a padded envelope.

Gift Parcel

Materials:

Washi tape: red paisley, narrow blue

Black solvent inkpad

White and red cardstock

Paper pack

Stickers

Black baker's twine

Black narrow ribbon

Mini white tag

Blank black card 11.5 x 16cm (4½ x 6¼in)

Foam mounting tape

Double-sided tape

Craft glue

Tools:

Small heart stamp

Instructions:

1 Cut an 8 x 6cm (3¼ x 2½in) piece of white cardstock. Place alternating strips of washi tape diagonally, leaving a narrow space between them. Trim off excess tape and ink the edges black. Wrap a piece of narrow black ribbon in the centre.

2 Cut an 8.5 x 2.2 (3⅜ x ⅞in) piece of red card and ink the edges. Wrap with narrow black ribbon. Use foam tape to attach it to the gift package, making sure the narrow black ribbons match up.

3 Cut an 11 x 8.5cm (4⅜ x 3⅜in) piece of white card and ink the edges. Wrap baker's twine around the top left and bottom right corners.

Wrap a short piece of baker's twine around the piece already at the bottom right and tie it in a knot. Use foam tape to attach the gift package in the centre.

4 Cut a 14 x 10cm (5½ x 3⅞in) piece of green patterned paper and ink the edges. Add a circle sticker in each corner. Mount on white cardstock with double-sided tape and attach to the card front. Use foam tape to attach the white cardstock piece in the centre.

5 Stamp the heart on the tag with black ink. Thread narrow black ribbon through the hole. Foam-tape to the top of the package. Tie a bow in a piece of baker's twine and use craft glue to secure at the top of the tag.

Christmas Gift Parcel

Washi tape gift parcels can be for birthdays, weddings, graduation – and Christmas! Simply add some metallic shine with gold striped washi tape and gold embroidery thread, then add a candy sweet stamp on the tiny tag for Christmas cheer.

Scallop Border

Materials:

Washi tape: purple/
  brown patchwork, solid
  narrow purple, solid
  narrow blue

Purple embossing
  powder

Embossing inkpad

Grey solvent inkpad

White cardstock

Paper flowers, small
  silk flower

Silver brads

Green grosgrain ribbon

Blank white card 12.7 x 16.5cm
  (5 x 6½in)

Double-sided tape

Craft glue

Tools:

Circle punch, 4.5cm (1¾in)

Vintage wallpaper stamp

Heat tool

Instructions:

1 Stamp the vintage wallpaper on white cardstock with embossing ink. Sprinkle with embossing powder and heat-set. Cut to 13 x 9cm (5¼ x 3½in) and ink the edges grey.

2 Place strips of washi tape on white cardstock, leaving a small space between each colour. Punch three circles from the piece and ink the edges grey. Cut two of the circles in half.

3 Glue three half-circles to the back edge of the embossed cardstock piece to create a scallop.

4 Wrap the piece with green ribbon. Place one half circle at the top of the ribbon edge and the other beneath it.

5 Layer the flowers together and insert a brad in each. Use foam tape to attach to the right side of the embossed piece.

6 Tie a bow in green ribbon and attach to the left side of the ribbon border with craft glue.

7 Cut a 14.5 x 10cm (5¾ x 4in) piece of white cardstock and ink the edges grey. Glue to the centre of the card front. Place strips of narrow blue washi tape overlapping on each corner. Use foam tape to attach the embossed piece in the centre.

Scallop Butterfly

Create scalloped borders on either side of your embossed piece – simply adjust how much of the circle shows on the front to make the scallops larger or smaller.

Heat-embossed Swirl

Materials:

Washi tape: solid turquoise, narrow pink, narrow brown

Wildflowers stamp set

Orange and teal patterned papers

White cardstock

Embossing inkpad

Gold embossing powder

Small gold border stickers

Dark turquoise grosgrain ribbon

Gold embroidery thread

Orange button

Brown solvent inkpad

Blank white card 12.7 x 16.5cm (5 x 6½in)

Foam mounting tape

Double-sided tape

Craft glue

Tools:

Heat tool

Swirl stamp

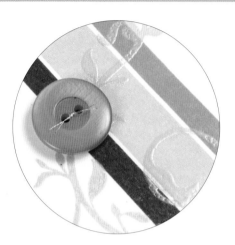

Instructions:

1 Place three strips of washi tape on an 11 x 14.5cm (4¼ x 5⅝in) piece of white card. Ink the edges brown. Stamp and heat-emboss the swirl with gold, then add gold circle stickers at each corner.

2 Mount the piece on orange patterned paper and ink the edges brown. Wrap with dark turquoise ribbon, securing the ends to the back with double-sided tape.

3 Cover the card front with teal patterned paper and ink the edges brown. Glue the mounted card focal in the centre.

4 Thread a button with gold embroidery thread and use foam tape to attach it to the card front. Tie a bow in dark turquoise ribbon and glue to the card front.

Heat-embossed Botanical
Choose another stamp to emboss in brown, using patterned washi tape for a background. With detailed stamps like this botanical, I find it is best to align the washi tape edges; with more free-form stamps like the swirl, you can leave a bit of space between them.

Feather Leaf Trio

Materials:

Washi tape: blue dot, purple/green patchwork, solid green

Book paper

Gold border stickers

Patterned papers

White acrylic paint

Green sheer ribbon

White and mauve cardstock

Silver embroidery thread

Brown solvent inkpad

Blank white card 12.7 x 16.5cm (5 x 6½in)

Foam mounting tape

Double-sided tape

Craft glue

Tools:

Feather template

Detail scissors

Paintbrush

Pencil

Instructions:

1 Cut a 7½ x 15¼cm (3 x 6in) piece of white card and fold lengthwise. Use the template to trace a large quail feather shape with a pencil, aligning the fold line of the feather shape with the fold of the paper. Then cut out the shape. Erase all the pencil lines, and place the folded card on your work surface.

2 Place the tape diagonally across the shape, starting at the top and leaving a small space between each pattern. Unfold and trim the excess with detail scissors. Fold the

piece again and repeat for the other side.

3 Trace and cut medium and small quail feathers and repeat the washi tape technique. Use foam tape to attach them to a 9.5 x 16.5cm (3¾ x 6½in) piece of green patterned paper. Ink the edges and mount on mauve card. Cover the seams with gold border stickers.

4 Cover the front of the card with light green patterned paper and ink the edges.

5 Paint a sheet of book paper with one coat of white acrylic

paint. Let it dry and tear the long edges. Attach the focal piece to the centre of the book paper with double-sided tape and wrap with green ribbon, securing the ends to the back.

6 Glue the piece to the card front. Thread a button with silver embroidery thread and attach it to the card front with foam tape. Then tie a knot in the green ribbon and glue it next to the button.

Trio of Feather Leaves

The Rule of Uneven Numbers is a great design trick; grouping embellishments in threes or fives is visually pleasing to the eye. You can overlap the grouping as in the main card (right), or space them out as I have done here (left). Note the alternating buttons and ribbon bow.

You are invited to visit the author's website:
www.saranaumann.com
for more information and video tutorials.

Acknowledgements
My thanks to Hot Off The Press/
Paper Wishes, WOW Embossing Powder,
Spellbinders, Clearsnap, We R Memory
Keepers, Kamoi/mt, Crafter's Companion
and The Crafter's Workshop for their
support with this book.